The Democratic Deficit

I0411979

Stephen C. Lovatt

The Democratic Deficit

CreateSpace

Seattle, WA. USA

ISBN-10: 1507881487
ISBN-13: 978-1507881484

First Edition (2015)

http://www.createspace.com

For Sammy, James and Erik

with whom I have often

crossed swords

Table of Contents

Ch 1   The Person and the State

'We should trust... especially the doctrine that the soul has an absolute superiority over the body, and that while I am alive I have nothing to thank for my individuality except my soul.' [Plato Laws (XII 959a)]

What is the meaning of life?

It seems to me that the direct answer to the question "what is the meaning of life" is: "life is that state of being in which a recognisable pattern or organisation of matter and/or energy persists as a result, not of static resistance to dissolution – as a diamond passively resits oxidation; but as emerging dynamically from a flux or flow of matter and/or energy, and which maintains its existence by systematically dumping entropy into this flux."[1]

This account of life certainly encompasses all plants, animals and bacteria which are currently categorised as "alive". Moreover it recognises that such carbon-based "organic" or "biological" life have a continuity with other physical phenomena such as candle-flames, whirl-pools and hurricanes. In all these cases there is a flux of matter and/or energy; whether this is "sun-light", or "evaporating wax", or "laminar water flow past the whirl-pool", or "convecting air".[2]

As far as politics is concerned, it is important to recognise that a society or community is a life-form in its own right: and one which subsists as a persistent organisation of those individual human beings, who themselves lend it material existence. An obvious comparison may be made between – on the one hand – an ant, bee, or wasp colony and – on the other hand – a human society, or community.

---

1   E. Schrödinger "What is Life?" (1992)
2   S. Lovatt "The Good of Being" Ch 4, p67-70.

What is a person?

It seems to me that a human person is not merely a singular instance of human nature, as a particular mushroom or rabbit is an individual example of the species to which it belongs. Rather, a human person is a spiritual or transcendent being which also has a material existence as an instantiation of a species of great ape. By "spiritual or transcendent being" I mean two distinct things which I believe are connected at a very deep level. A spiritual or transcendent being is, first: *aware* of reality as a *consciously experiencing subject;*[3] and, second: has some *eternal dimension to its existence.*[4] It is important to make the spiritual or transcendent character of human beings explicit, as this is the ontological basis of "inalienable human rights."

The first characteristic means much more than "displays behaviour indicative of feelings, emotions, memory, reason and a recognition of self." Consciousness is an aspect of reality which is necessarily personal and subjective. Hence, it is impossible to speak of consciousness except by means of altogether inadequate analogies; still less is consciousness measurable. The second characteristic does not necessarily signify "life after death". It might mean "makes a significant contribution to the never-ending story of the human race"; if only the Second Law of Thermodynamics did not tell us that all physical things are futile, ending in decay and dissolution.

What is the state?

The word "state" can be used synonymously with "society" or "community"; but it can also have a particular connotation, namely: those aspects of a society which govern it, especially with regards to its external defence and internal policing. "The state" is more than simply the "government" or "executive", as it also includes whatever legislature, consultative assembly, judiciary, military and police force the society incorporates. If there is a

---

3   S. Lovatt "The Good of Being" Ch 6, p99-108.
4   S. Lovatt "The Good of Being" Ch 9, p167-169.

close connection between an established religion and the government then "the state" also incorporates that religion.

In this second use of the word "state", it is possible to view "the state" as nothing other than an overwhelmingly dominant protection racket; which provides order and security to those within its control in return for extorted levies – otherwise known as duties, charges, licence fees and taxes. This doesn't mean that "the state" is necessarily malign. The "protection racket" might be run by a fairly decent "God Father" or "Mafia Council" and serve the common interest of its clientele well; but this does not alter the fact that in its origin "the state" is merely the individual or group of individuals that has gained power over a community by one means or another.

Anarchy

Anarchism is the absence of any state in the second sense; each individual being responsible for and to only themselves. It is the political equivalent of unbridled free market economics. While such a system might be practical for a small community, it becomes impractical once even a moderate number of people congregate together. Every dispute has to be resolved on its own terms, among the parties concerned. This is liable to degenerate into violent conflict and the dominance of the strong over the weak. In the absence of general rules and agreed norms of behaviour there is no basis for the protection of the vulnerable, or for the maintenance of property rights; and anarchy is liable to degenerate into "devil take the hindmost" banditry.

Totalitarianism

Totalitarianism originally meant an "all embracing state". It is the antithesis of Anarchism. The label has been pejoratively applied to a wide variety of regimes. In particular, Popper contrasts it with Democracy. He argued that totalitarianism arises from the false teleological notion that history is moving toward an immutable future in according to knowable laws.[5] The most familiar examples of totalitarianism are Fascism and Marxism.

---

5   K.R. Popper "The Poverty of Historicism" (1957)

Tyranny and dictatorship

Tyranny is often confused with dictatorship. Indeed, Popper uses the terms interchangeably.[6] Nevertheless, in common usage the two are not the same. Whereas a tyrant is always a dictator; the converse is not true. A tyrant is a ruler who uses his power for some improper purpose[7] to the detriment of the people whom he rules. A tyrant is not concerned with justice. A tyrant may rule a totalitarian state, but tyranny is more to do with the intention and character of the rule rather than whether or not it is all-encompassing. A tyrant cannot be benevolent, and will not be sustainably popular; whereas a dictator or king may be either or both.

---

6   See Ch 7.
7   Such as self-aggrandizement, the accumulation of personal wealth, or the pursuit of some inhumane political theory.

Ch 2 What is Democracy?

'The majority I disregard.' [Plato "Gorgias" (474a)]

Democracy is supposedly "rule by the demos or common folk." As pure Democracy is impractical except in the smallest of communities, Democracy generally occurs in its "representative" form; where a set of chosen individuals are supposed to speak and/or act for the common folk. Representative Democracy is no more than that system of government in which laws are enacted by majority vote in a legislative assembly of such persons.

Representatives are not necessarily elected by the common folk. They need only be recognised or deemed in some way to be representative of the demos. Moreover, the election of representatives by the common folk does not guarantee that they will be in any way *representative* of the common folk, in the sense of being a faithful sample. Often, elected representatives are male rather than female and much more affluent, articulate and better educated than the norm. They also tend to be lawyers, or even full-time politicians, rather than of any other trade or profession.[1]

There is no mechanism for minority views to be heeded in such a system, so its critics characterize it as giving rise to "the tyranny of the majority". It is entirely possible for a society to be totally democratic (in the sense that its government is regularly elected in "free and fair" elections by a majority of the common folk) and in practice be an oppressive police state. At root, all that Democracy consists of is the identification of rightness or legitimacy with electoral might: which amounts to the force of votes, rather than the force of arms.

---

1 These are simply facts. I do not mean to insinuate that these facts are either deplorable or undesirable, on the one hand; or that that they are either insignificant or beneficial, on the other.

Multi-party Democracy

Multi-party Democracy is the system of government according to which laws are approved by the majority vote of a set of politicians, elected or appointed according to some procedure or other. Left to themselves, politicians typically gang together into factional voting blocks called "parties". The members of each party generally vote together in accordance with either the instruction of their leaders, or else some other internal decision making process.

Single-party Democracy

In a *single party Democracy* laws are formally enacted by democratic procedures; with the proviso that all those voting are members of a single faction or party, and are under the supervision and control of the leadership of that faction. Such a system is indistinguishable from an Oligarchy, with the criterion for membership of the governing clique being loyalty to the party. In a single party Democracy the legislature is bound to be the creature of the party executive. Both Marxist and Fascist states tend to present themselves as single party Democracies.

Non-partisan Democracy

In a *non-partisan* Democracy the legislature is either composed of individuals who are forbidden from forming long-standing formal alliances; or else is governed by rules which render such factional alliances impractical. A system of pure Democracy (in which every decision is made by plebiscite) would pretty much conform to this prescription; as, perhaps, does the (non elected) parliament of Saudi Arabia. In a non-partisan Democracy either the executive will appoint the legislature and therefore dominate it, even in the absence of any party structure as such; or else the executive will be weak: being unable to manage a disparate and chaotic legislature.

Accountability

It is vital to distinguish "accountability" from "Democracy". Those in authority can, and should, be held to account against various criteria, in various forums and according to various mechanisms. Democracy amounts to the three ideas:

1. Only one forum matters: the general population, or its supposed representatives.
2. Only one mechanism is legitimate: balloting.
3. Only one criterion matters: a simple majority.

What Democracy is not

One must be careful not to confuse Democracy with "humane attitudes", "individual liberty", "freedom of speech", "minority rights", or "the rule of law" and so on. A society might feature all of these values without there being any element of Democracy present within it. Indeed, Democracy can in principle result – and has in practice resulted – in the compromising of such values. All that is required for injustice to win out is for a majority of the common people to be ill-educated or otherwise prejudiced.

Other political ideas which are not democratic as such are: "egalitarianism", "tolerance", "fair shares for all", "hand-outs for the poor", "the celebration of cultural diversity", "progressive taxation", "comprehensive education", "the welfare state", "redistribution of wealth", and so on. Some of these paradigms have a consonance with Democracy, for they are liable to be perceived by a majority of the common folk as being in their immediate selfish interest, and therefore to be popular; but this does not make them democratic. They are at most policies that one might anticipate a Democracy to adopt, and this anticipation amounts to no kind of approval of such policies.

Ch 3   Alternatives to Democracy

'The proper object of true political skill is not the interest
of private individuals but the common good... then the
individual and the community alike are benefited.'
[Plato "Laws" (IX 875b)]

Granted that tyranny (in the normal sense of the word) is to be
avoided; a variety of alternative political arrangements are
regularly proposed as providing for this objective.

Libertarianism

Libertarianism is the idea that individuals should be free to do
what they wish, as long as they do not infringe on the liberty of
others. It is therefore a type of minimally regulated anarchism.
Some Libertarians regard all initiation of force as immoral and
would rely on self-policing to maintain this principle. These are
indistinguishable from pacifist Anarchists: "Hippies", if you like.
Others, of a more Objectivist[1] bent, support the establishment
of a limited state which exercises the minimum amount of force,
according to law, deemed necessary to protect and guarantee
individual freedom.

Aristocracy

Aristocracy literally means "the rule of the best". An Aristocracy
generally claims to be dedicated to the common good. "Best"
is then implicitly defined as "most able to provide for the common
good". An Aristocracy need not be hereditary, in which case
it is better styled a Meritocracy. Unfortunately, Aristocracies
have a tendency to degenerate into hereditary Oligarchies[2]
or Plutocracies,[3] in which "best" means nothing more than
a particular set of families who have come – for no good reason –
to be thought of as somehow "superior" to the rest of society.

---

1   The individualist philosophy of Ayn Rand.
2   Rule by an establishment or "in-crowd".
3   Rule by the wealthy.

Monarchy

A Monarchy is an Aristocracy in which a single person (or, occasionally, a pair of people) has a crucial and definitive role in government. It is usual for the Monarch(s) to hold office until death; though this is not part of the definition of monarchy.

'A king is the people's only protection against tyranny – especially against the worst of all tyrants, themselves.[4] "Prof" will be ideal for the job – because he does not want the job.' [R.A. Heinlein "The Moon is a harsh mistress" (1966, 1969)]

A Monarchy need be neither hereditary nor absolute. It is entirely possible to have a Monarchy which is constrained by convention or constitutional law.[5] An important characteristic of Monarchy is that it is natural for a monarch (at least of the hereditary variety) to take the long view; to be concerned with future generations: the well-being of their dynasty, as well as their own present well-being. A monarch is not immediately answerable to any electorate, nor required to produce short-term results; though any extended deficiency of rule is liable to produce disaffection and rebellion among their subjects.

A good monarchical system grooms each king or queen in waiting, seeking to inculcate in them an acute sense of duty and of history; of personal responsibility to justice, and the preservation – both now and into the future – of liberty, culture and custom. A Monarchy is therefore more adept at responding to strategic problems (such as globalization, climate change, population growth, unsustainable development and environmental despoliation) than any democratic administration; which is bound to find it difficult to plan beyond the next general election.

---

4   The common folk can tyrannise themselves by enacting policies which they believe to be in their best interests but which actually harm them.

5   Whereas dictatorship is often absolute in character and claims freedom from all regulation, constraint and law – basing this claim on a supposed expertise and competence.

'I have a trust committed to me by God, by old and lawful descent, I will not betray it, to answer a new unlawful authority... I do stand more for the liberty of my people, than any here that come to be my pretended judges... I will stand as much for the privilege of the House of Commons, rightly understood, as any man here...

I am sworn to keep the peace, by that duty I owe to God and my country; and I will do it to the last breath of my body... It was [for] the liberty, freedom, and laws of the subject that ever I took – defended myself with arms. I never took up arms against the people, but for the laws...

It is the liberty of the people of England that I stand for. For me to acknowledge a new Court that I never heard of before – I that am your King, that should be an example to all the people of England, for to uphold justice, to maintain the old laws – indeed I do not know how to do it.' [Charles I "Defence before the House of Commons" (1649)]

Theocracy

This term seems to mean "rule by God", but in practice it always means "rule by priests"; where the priesthood is a group of Oligarchs who claim to have an understanding of morality, history and statecraft which is beyond that of the common people.

Communism and Socialism

Communism is an ambiguous term, meaning anything from simply "holding goods in common", as is the case for monastics; to a totalitarian regime, in which the able are required to work for no commensurate reward and the incompetent are given everything they demand.

Communism can work when the people involved are well motivated by either friendship[6] or profound devotion to a common cause, such as a religious vocation; but in the absence of love

---

6   It is on this basis that Plato recommends Communism in "Republic".

and personal virtue it is bound to degenerate into lethargy, unless it is enforced by some kind of Leninist totalitarianism.

Socialism is either the name by which Communism goes when coupled with some form of Democracy; or else a watered-down doctrine which allows a limited level of private property, while demanding that "the means of production" (typically, heavy industry and public transport) should be nationalised.

Neither Communism nor Socialism is an alternative to Democracy; being merely specific economic paradigms which a state (democratic or otherwise) might adopt.

Marxism

The philosopher Hegel proposed a form of Idealism in which the attainment of perfect freedom is the destiny of human history. He believed that for every "thesis" in the history of human thought there arises a contradictory "antithesis". In the ensuing conflict – or "dielectic" – a "synthesis" is formed; which itself elicits a new "antithesis" and so on: until perfection is achieved.[7]

Marx's early writings were a response to these ideas. While maintaining the idea of inevitable progress through conflict, Marx inverted Hegel's idealistic dialectic; arguing that material circumstances shape ideas, instead of the other way around. Marx insisted that social development springs from the contradictions inherent to material life. He believed that primitive communism developed into slave states; which then grew into feudal societies. These in turn had become capitalist states, which would finally be replaced by one single socialist state.

Marx did not found his anthropology on an understanding of the human individual. Instead he began with society. He claimed that individualism was a social disease resulting from an obsession with property, and the alienation of the person from their true role as a constituent of society. He thought that the socialist state should not concern itself primarily with issues like liberty and equality; but with the abolition of private property, which he took to be the root cause of individualism.

---

7   This is a generalisation of Plato's notion that dialogue between two antagonists might obtain truth by a fruitful refinement of ideas.

Marxism as such does not represent a polity, any more than Communism or Socialism; however its emphasis on revolutionary change implies a totalitarian government. This is evinced by the term "Dictatorship of the Proletariat"; which can only mean the establishment in power of some person or group claiming to act for the common folk – on the basis of a Marxist account of economics, morality and history. Hence, Marxism is a pretext for the establishment of an "atheistic theocracy".

Fascism

Fascism correctly conceives of the state (in the primary sense of a community or nation) as a living thing, it wrongly attributes to the state a personal consciousness, which it fails to distinguish from that of an experiential moral subject.

> The Fascist State is itself conscious and has itself a will and a personality.
> [B. Mussolini and G. Gentile "Fascism" (1932)]

Fascism considers that individuals and associations of individuals – such as the Church – have only existence and significance relative to the state, and is a pretext for the establishment of a theocratic meritocracy.[8]

> Fascism has created a living faith; and that this faith is very powerful in the minds of men is demonstrated by those who have suffered and died for it.
> [B. Mussolini and G. Gentile "Fascism" (1932)]

Fascism rejects the notion that the state exists for the benefit of the individual citizens, and attributes to the state rights which transcend and overwhelm any rights which a human individual might be thought to possess. It denies that the common people have any role in directing human society, and affirms the basic inequality of individual human beings; which it claims to see as beneficial and fruitful. Fascism has little time for liberty.

---

8   In the Twentieth Century it only gave rise to totalitarian oligarchies.

> The Fascist State organizes the nation, but leaves a
> sufficient margin of liberty to the individual; the latter
> is deprived of all useless and possibly harmful freedom.[9]
> [B. Mussolini and G. Gentile "Fascism" (1932)]

This view of society can be understood as an misapplication
of Catholic Ecclesiology to the secular arena. Although
Catholic theology does not subjugate the individual to the
collective; the Church is viewed as being the Body of Christ,
and so as having a personal subjective experiential consciousness:
that of Jesus of Nazareth. Similarly, the Catholic leadership
is very keen to distinguish between useful and harmful liberties.

Capitalism

Capitalism is the idea that human beings should be allowed, first,
to accumulate personal wealth by means of their skill, ingenuity
and effort; and, second, to trade goods and services with others
by means of a free market. Arguably, this economic system is a
natural concomitant of Democracy; and is certainly no more an
alternative to Democracy than is Socialism. It is, nevertheless,
often denounced by Socialists as "undemocratic", on the basis that
wealthy people form a minority with power (accruing from their
wealth) which is out of proportion with their numbers.

Lottocracy

Every political decision could be made by use of a lottery;
with each proposed policy option being given a chance of
becoming law in strict proportion to its popularity. The obvious
advantage of this polity is that no one majority party would
be able to dominate. Indeed, this is arguably the ultimate form
of "proportional representation". The obvious disadvantage
attendant on this arrangement is that sometimes very unpopular,
extremist and/or foolish decisions are bound to be arrived at.

---

9   No reasonable person could want anything that was truly "useless"
    or "harmful"; but the implication here is that almost all liberty
    and free speech is "useless" and "harmful".

Modern Feudalism

As another alternative to Democracy, consider a segmented state run by competing feudal lords who recruit vassals by offering them forms and practices of governance which it is intended they will find attractive. Clearly, this would be inefficient (because the state would be divided into many parallel jurisdictions) but just as clearly, the officers of such a state would be acutely accountable to the population. If any of them did something unpopular among their followers, they would find it difficult to retain any of them; their vassals would simply transfer allegiance to an alternate lord.

Enforced Power Sharing

A significant variant of Democracy has been implemented in the United Kingdom. Northern Ireland has a "power-sharing" Executive. The rules according to which the members of the province's government are appointed guarantee that all parties with any significant popularity are represented, as a kind of forced "grand coalition". This means that political enemies have to negotiate and work together at all times; rather than the majority party having all the power.

The United States of America

The United States is not, properly speaking, democratic. This is because its written constitution significantly constrains Congress; and the Supreme Court can squash any democratically enacted law simply by ruling that it is unconstitutional.

Ch 4   The case for Democracy

'Well then, Alcibiades, what about a city? What is it that
is present and what will be absent when a city is in a
better condition and getting better management and
treatment?'
  'The way that I look at it, Socrates, mutual friendship
will be present and hatred and insurrection will be absent.'
[Plato "Alcibiades" (126b-c)]

There are two distinguishable arguments in favour of Democracy.
The first seeks to establish that this form of government is itself
a positive good, and that it is bound to have salutary effects
wherever it is adopted and faithfully followed. The second
is more restrained. It seeks only to recommend Democracy
as being a partial means to a limited end. The first argument
is favoured by Neoconservatives and the second by Liberals.

The Neoconservative's positive justification

The Neoconservative position is based on the replacement of the
sovereignty of kings by the sovereignty of the common people.
From this, it is deduced that all authority in the state derives
upwards from the collective, rather than downwards from the
king. In the absence of unanimity of view, the exercise of this
collective authority requires some kind of decision making
process based on voting.

  Neoconservatism is generally combined with a belief
in "the Natural Law". This justifies the presumption that the
instincts of "the silent majority" are generally sound; and will,
in the end, support whatever kind of social and political
programme is supported by the Neoconservative – especially if
enough media coverage is bought.

  The Neoconservative typically presumes that Democracy
pulls society together in two ways. First, by encouraging people to
engage in political debate, which is accounted as a good thing;
and second, by forcing leaders to moderate their policies in

pursuit of votes "in the centre ground of politics"; which is where he likes to think that he lives. The Neoconservative is therefore willing to abide by the will of the majority. Even when they get it wrong in his eyes, he thinks it is better to give way to the majority view than to accept the diktat of some aristocracy or oligarchy; which is also liable to be mistaken and may be less amenable to persuasion.

The Neoconservative also assumes that democratic states are liable to be friendly towards each other, because they will have similar outlooks and compatible policy objectives. It was on this basis that the USA attempted to introduce Democracy into Iraq and Afghanistan; the idea being that Democracy is a stronger ideology than Islam and would act to moderate and tame Islam's more fanatical and fundamentalist tendencies.

The Liberal's negative justification

The Liberal is, at first sight, a natural democrat. This is because he believes that each person "has their own truth" and that each is accountable to none other than himself. Hence, in the necessity of social living the only conceivable means by which rules and norms can be established is by consensus; or, failing that, the will of some representative group: most plausibly the majority.

The Liberal is not at all sure that individual liberty (which is what matters supremely to him) is guaranteed by the mere existence of a democratic process. He is well aware that bigotry is a powerful force in human society, and has regularly overwhelmed mankind's more humanitarian and enlightened instincts. The popularity of lynchings, pogroms, and witch trials bears sad testimony to this fact. He is well aware that in a democratic system – such as to some extent exists in both the USA and UK – liberal attitudes (which he believes to be the very basis of wholesome governance) are regularly opposed and often defeated by what he judges to be reactionary forces.

The Liberal acknowledges that in a representative Democracy, the government is something of an "elected oligarchy". In the absence of a written constitution, such a government is more or less able to do whatsoever it wills. Even in a state with a decent constitution and an independent Supreme Court to uphold it, the executive and legislature still have a good deal of freedom. This is because the time scales on which they can act are much shorter than that on which the judiciary can react. It therefore seems desirable to provide a means of summarily deposing a bad government without resorting to violence. Typically, this is going to be by some sort of electoral process.

The Liberal views the Neoconservative's justification of Democracy uneasily. He detects in it the idea that Democracy is only "true Democracy" if the Neoconservative likes what it results in. For the Neoconservative, this is not an issue; as for him this is inevitable, given his belief in the universality of "common-sense values". In the end, the Liberal may admit that Democracy is not particularly good; but argue that as no-one has ever proposed a better system, one must simply make the best of a bad job.

Democracy is the worst form of government, except for all those other forms that have been tried from time to time. [W. Churchill "Speech in the House of Commons" (11th November 1947)]

Popper's demarcation

Both of the above arguments are beset by difficulties.

1. The idea of "sovereignty" is suspect as a starting place for any argument. To decide who should be sovereign on the basis that someone has to be, is at best naive. It would rather be better to first ask what sovereignty is and what purpose it serves, and only then proceed to consider how it should be exercised.
2. The word "authority" is ambiguous. It can mean anything from arbitrary coercive power, to real and demonstrated expertise.
3. The fact that a group of people cannot agree on something is no basis for imposing the will of the majority on the minority.
4. It is unclear why the tyranny of the majority is to be preferred to that of an individual or oligarchy.
5. It is unclear how the majority can be expected to "be right".

6. Experience suggests that Democracy is just as liable to
polarize society and produce discord as to facilitate harmony
and good order. Obvious examples are Northern Ireland, Libya,
Zimbabwe, Nigeria and Iraq.
7. Democracy is not so much an ideology as a mechanism.
8. The fact that Democracy allows for the peaceful deposition
of a bad government does not mean that there is no better system.
9. Indeed, to judge a system entirely in terms of how it deals
with its own failures seems to be a council of despair.
10. What is meant by the judgement "bad government" any-how,
and how is such a state of affairs to be identified?

A particular version of the liberal argument in favour of
Democracy has been proposed by Popper. In an attempt to answer
at least some of the questions listed in the previous paragraph and
to make his case rigorous, he first divests Democracy of its
normal meaning – relating to either the will of the majority or else
rule by the common people – redefining "democratic system"
as "a system in which the rulers can dismissed by 'the ruled'
by any means other than bloodshed."

> For we may distinguish two main types of government.
> The first type consists of governments of which we can
> get rid of without bloodshed – for example, by way of
> general elections; that is to say, the social institutions
> provide means by which the rulers may be dismissed
> by the ruled, and the social traditions ensure that these
> institutions will not easily be destroyed by those who are
> in power. The second type consists of governments which
> the ruled cannot get rid of except by way of a successful
> revolution – that is to say, in most cases, not at all.
> I suggest the term 'Democracy' as a short-hand label for a
> government of the first type, and the term 'tyranny' or
> 'dictatorship'; for the second.
> [K.R. Popper "The Spell of Plato" Ch 7 (1945)]

This is unobjectionable, so far as it goes. After all what Popper proposes here is no more than a convention of word usage; a demarcation seemingly akin to the fruitful one which he had already developed to distinguish Physics from Metaphysics.[1] However, one must be aware that the definitions which he is proposing are counter to all normal use, and that one of his terms is pejorative.[2]

The deficit in Popper's political demarcation

> If we make use of the two labels as suggested, then we can now describe, as the principle of a democratic policy, the proposal to create, develop, and protect political institutions for the avoidance of tyranny. This principle does not imply that we can ever develop institutions of this kind which are faultless or foolproof, or which ensure that the policies adopted by a democratic government will be right or good or wise – or even necessarily better or wiser than the policies adopted by a benevolent tyrant. (Since no such assertions are made, the paradox of Democracy is avoided.)
> [K.R. Popper "The Spell of Plato" Ch 7 (1945)]

Popper's "paradox of Democracy is avoided", but only formally, by defining it away. Up to this point in his argument, the idea that "Democracy" is preferable to "tyranny" – with Popper's use of these words – has not featured. However, this cannot continue. For his political demarcation to have any motive or rationale, this deficit now has to be supplied.

---

1   K.R. Popper "The Logic of Scientific Discovery" (1934, 1968)
2   In ordinary usage, an oligarchy or Democracy can be described as tyrannical, even in the absence of an identifiable tyrant. Ironically, a system in which the composition of the government is determined by some form of financial auction would – according to Popper – count as "democratic"; and a humane, popular, responsible, consultative and kind monarchy would count as "tyrannical".

What may be said, however, to be implied in the adoption
of the democratic principle is the conviction that the
acceptance of even a bad policy in a Democracy (as long
as we can work for a peaceful change) is preferable to the
submission to a tyranny, however wise or benevolent.
[K.R. Popper "The Spell of Plato" Ch 7 (1945)]

It seems that Popper's over-riding view is that "tyranny"
(on his definition of the term) is the paramount political evil,
and should be opposed at all cost – even at the cost of establishing
objective wickedness! According to this "conviction", it would
be right to work for the overthrow of a benign monarch – whose
every policy was just, wise, moderate and compassionate –
in order to establish a Democracy; even one in which it was
clearly envisaged that corruption, oppression and cruelty would
abound! I cannot think this is what Popper really believed;
but rather that he had faith that "the people can be trusted"
and that Democracy would, in the end, produce good results.
In other words, I think that he was a Neoconservative, only posing
as a Liberal.

He who accepts the principle of Democracy in this sense
is therefore not bound to look upon the result of a
democratic vote as an authoritative expression of what is
right. Although he will accept a decision of the majority,
for the sake of making the democratic institutions work,
he will feel free to combat it by democratic means,
and to work for its revision. And should he live to see the
day when the majority vote destroys the democratic
institutions, then this sad experience will tell him only
that there does not exist a foolproof method of avoiding
tyranny. But it need not weaken his decision to fight
tyranny, nor will it expose his theory as inconsistent.
[K.R. Popper "The Spell of Plato" Ch 7 (1945)]

Whatever might be meant by the phrases "good government"
and "bad government", Popper concedes here that there is no
reason to believe that Democracy will promote justice.

After all, democratic institutions can be no more righteous or noble than the mass of the population. What is the virtue in the common people replacing a government which is good, but unpopular, with one that is bad, but popular? Of itself, Popper's "Democracy" is a prescription for nothing other than "government by beauty contest" and endemic instability.

In summary, Popper replaces the question "Who shall rule?" with the stipulation that "Whoever rules, they must be readily disposable." He answers the "authority" question by asserting that the common people have the absolute right to depose their governors, who only rule with their consent. Indeed, it would seem that "good" must be equated with "popular" and "bad" with "unpopular" – at least as far as the criterion for appointing and dismissing rulers is concerned.

Popper attempts to justify the tyranny of the majority by presenting an unjustified "conviction" that it is preferable to the tyranny of the few. He claims that no political decision can have anything other than a provisional character, though in fact some are pretty much irreversible; and that no political decision can justifiably claim to be "right", yet insinuates that democratic decisions will tend to "get it right".

Popper's analysis is fundamentally flawed. This is because (unlike his demarcation of Physics from Metaphysics, which distinguishes two good things from each other) his demarcation of "Democracy" from "tyranny" is supposed to distinguish a good thing from a bad one. It is therefore an attempt to produce moral value by linguistic sleight of hand. It fails to do so, because such an enterprise is fundamentally impossible.

Ch 5   The case against Democracy

'Extreme freedom can't be expected to lead to anything
but a change to extreme slavery, whether for a private
individual or for a city... tyranny evolves from...
Democracy – the most severe and cruel slavery from
the utmost freedom.' [Plato "Republic" (VIII 564a)]

The will of the majority does not welcome constraint; whether
of constitution, judicial review, human rights convention or
ecclesiastical sanction. When "what the electorate wants"
conflicts with "what is objectively right", it is a foolhardy
politician who sides with justice. Democracy tends to mistake
law for justice, and legality with righteousness. The majority
comes to believe that it is *right* for it enact whatever law
it see fit; whether it is wise or foolish, equitable or cruel.

'Their very ignorance of their true state fixes them the
more firmly therein. For they do not know what is the
penalty of injustice, which is the last thing of which a
man should be ignorant.' [Plato "Theaetetus" (177d)]

On occasion, democratic majorities have overturned great
injustices. Obvious examples are the abolition of the African
slave trade, the emancipation of the North American slaves
and the final success of the civil rights movement in the USA.
Nevertheless, democratic majorities are also liable to impose
injustices, as in the criminalization of both Catholicism and
homosexuality in the UK. Democracy is not concerned,
at its core, with what is *right* and *needful*; but with what is
popular: what the voter *wants*.

In a Democracy, manslaughter could be decriminalized;[1]
two teenagers holding hands be made illegal[2] and promiscuity

---

1   In both the UK and USA, abortion and euthanasia are increasingly
    common.
2   This is now arguably the case in the UK, but the law is not enforced.

be subsidized by the state[3] Without some standard or authority other than the will of the majority, Democracy makes justice into whatever the mob wants it to be.

> 'If it were only my own particular case, I would have satisfied myself with the protestation I made the last time I was here... but it is not my case alone, it is the freedom and the liberty of the people of England; and do you pretend what you will, I stand more for their liberties. For if power without law, may make laws, may alter the fundamental laws of the Kingdom, I do not know what subject he is in England that can be sure of his life, or any thing that he calls his own.' [Charles I "Defence before the House of Commons" (1649)]

Party politics is especially wicked when groups form on the basis, not of shared ideals, but with the aim of maintaining vested interests. British party politics has always been organized along these lines. The Whigs were the party of the quasi-republican, Puritan and legalistic merchants; the Tories were the party of the royalist, Catholic and libertarian land-owners. The Whigs then became the Liberals. They were then sidelined by the emerging Labour party, which was at first the party of the Methodist trades unions; but more recently, as "New Labour", itself became "Whiggish" in character as it sought to obtain the votes of the increasingly affluent, numerous and self-important "middle class".

Political expertise

It is not a good thing that authority should be accountable to the general population. Any sensible type of accountability works the other way round. It makes some agency that is responsible for making day-to-day decisions answerable to some *expert* authority. The need to do this arises when the expert authority has delegated the responsibility for making

---

3   The extensive system of social support available in the UK to single mothers is an incentive for young women to become pregnant in order to qualify for state subsidy.

decisions to a lesser agency. It is extremely foolhardy to make an agency accountable to some body which has no expertise to evaluate that agency's actions, and so cannot judge its performance *rationally* – on the basis of understanding.

Were a group of wise experts trying to decide on a course of action driven by circumstances to ballot on some matter, they would not each opt for what they personally desired; but rather vote for what they dispassionately and honestly believed to be the best option. Those who loose the vote will believe that the wrong decision was made, but will not feel personally aggrieved.

In the case of a democratic vote, the common people[4] cannot vote on the basis of an expertise which they do not possess. Hence, they can only vote on the basis of desire, never according to what they dispassionately and honestly judge to be best; for if they were honest in their judgement they would have to admit that they really didn't know. Those who loose out will feel that they have been lumbered with something which they didn't want at all.

The retail paradigm

Everywhere in today's Britain, people are being called "customers" and all services (whether in the private or public sectors) are being organized so as to give their customers "choice". In effect, every aspect of human intercourse is being re-constructed on the lines of a shop-keeper's commercial relationship with his customer. This analogy is natural to the Whig mentality. The relationship between merchant and customer is simple. The will of the customer is necessarily the sole measure by which the merchant is judged. After all, the business of the successful merchant is nothing other than to supply his customer with what they want – or can be induced to want by advertising.

The "expertise" characteristic of a customer is nothing other than their "desire". Everyone knows well enough what they subjectively *want*, even if they have no idea at all of what they

---

4   Among which the author counts himself.

objectively *need*. Hence, the customer is always competent in their role as customer. They infallibly act according to their "expert knowledge" of their wants and desires. Only if they intend to re-sell the commodity which they are thinking of purchasing do they need to have any appreciation of its "true worth". Even then, this amounts to no more than an estimate of the price at which they think they could sell it on to another customer.

Plato's critique of Democracy

Plato preferred a different analogy: the relationship of the doctor (or other professional) with a client. This relationship is complicated. While it is the client who pays, and the client who has the final say; the professional acts autonomously towards, or on behalf of the client: in accordance with their own judgement of what the client objectively needs. Frequently, this is contrary to the client's immediate desire and inclination.

> 'Do you think that when people do something, they want the thing that they're doing at the time, or the thing for the sake of which they do what they're doing? Do you think that people who take medicine proscribed by their doctors, for instance, want what they're doing – the act of taking the medicine, with all its discomfort – or do they want to be healthy; the thing for the sake of which they're taking it?' [Plato "Gorgias" (467c]

While the client may not enjoy the process, they acknowledge that it must be undergone for their own long-term good. The client who ignores the advice or instruction of the expert is foolhardy. Generally, the client has to trust the skill, judgement and integrity of the professional whom they are employing. They should base this trust on the manifest coherence of what the expert says, on the testimonial of their teacher and mentor, and on the recommendation of their previous clients.[5]

---

5   Plato "Gorgias" (514a-e)

What person, when confronted by a difficult decision or urgent need, would seek advice or instruction from an arbitrary member of the public?

> 'When there is a question of the sweetness and dryness of the next vintage, I presume it would always be the grower's judgement that would carry authority, rather than that of a musician... again, in any question of what will be in tune or out of tune, would the judgement of a teacher of gymnastics be superior to that of a musician – even about what is going to seem in tune to the gymnastics master himself?'
> [Plato "Theaetetus" (178d)]

Still less would they accept medical or surgical intervention from someone without the appropriate education and experience. It would be no wiser to consult with a group representative of the population at large. Although a minority of these might happen to be experts, their voices would be lost in the clamour of the rabble.

> 'I don't really suppose that you [Callicles] think that two are better than one, or that your slaves are better than you just because they're stronger than you... Won't you say whether by "the better" and "the superior" you mean "the more intelligent"?'
> 'Yes, by Zeus, they're very much the ones I mean.'
> 'So on your reasoning it will often be the case that a single intelligent person is superior to countless unintelligent ones; that this person should rule and they be ruled...'
> 'Yes, that's what I do mean. This is what I take the just by nature to be: that the better one – the more intelligent one, that is, both rules over and has a greater share than his inferiors.'
> [Plato "Gorgias" (489d-490a)]

Democracy is founded on dishonesty

The skill of a democratic politician is primarily dissimulation. He wants to obtain power for himself. He may attempt to justify this in terms of some noble objective which he wishes to fulfil; but even so, the actual task set before him is to accumulate enough votes to be elected. He is best advised to do this by considering his market, asking himself what it is that people want to hear, and figuring out how he can either present his true programme so that it will be mistaken for this; or else adapt it so that in fact it conforms to what the market is demanding.

> 'You keep shifting back and forth [Callicles]. If you say anything in the Assembly and the populous of Athens denies it; you shift your ground and say what it wants to hear.' [Plato "Gorgias" (481e)]

Above all, he should bear in mind that what will convince others is not what is true, but rather what is plausible.

> 'Tisius wrote that if a weak but spunky man is taken to court because he beat up a strong but cowardly one... neither should tell the truth. The coward must say that the spunky man had accomplices, while the defendant must... fall back on that well-worn plea: 'How could a weak man like me attack a strong man like him?' The strong man, naturally, will not admit his cowardice.'
> [Plato "Phaedrus" (273c)]

He would be unwise to seek to convince the electorate to support his true aims. Even if he is motivated by some noble end, it would be unwise to present this too insistently: it is liable to alienate more voters than it will recruit. Almost certainly he will have to obtain the votes of people who want different (usually incompatible) things from him, and perhaps of people he personally despises. He will be forced to do this by presenting different messages to various audiences, and hoping that it will not be noticed that they conflict until after he has won power.

'It is not necessary for the intending orator to learn what is really just, but only what will seem just to the crowd who will act as judges. Nor again what is really good and noble, but only what will seem so. For that is what persuasion proceeds from, not truth.'
[Plato "Phaedrus" (260a)]

Hence the democratic politician is a professional flatterer; either by personal bent, or else by pressure of circumstance.

'I think that there's a practice that's not craft-like, but one that a mind given to making hunches takes to, a mind that's bold and naturally clever at dealing with people. I call it flattery, basically... I call oratory a part of this, too, along with cosmetics and sophistry...

By my reasoning, oratory is an image of a part of politics... it's a shameful thing... In politics, the counterpart of gymnastics[6] is legislation,[7] and the part that corresponds to medicine[6] is justice[7]...

Now flattery takes notice of them and... divides itself into four, masks itself with each of the parts and then pretends to be the characters of the masks. It takes no thought at all of whatever is best...

Pastry-baking has put on the mask of medicine... it guesses at what's pleasant with no consideration for what's best. And I say it is not a craft, but a knack – because it has no account of the nature of whatever things it applies... so that it's unable to state the cause of each thing...

Cosmetics is the flattery that wears the mask of gymnastics... so as to make people assume an alien beauty and neglect their own, which comes through gymnastics... you follow me now... that what pastry-baking is to medicine, oratory is to justice.'
[Plato "Gorgias" (463a-466a)]

---

6   For the body.
7   For the soul.

Democracy leads to Demagogy

Because of this, Democracy inevitably leads to demagogy.[8] It may either do so quickly, or else take its time; it may do so directly, or else in fits and starts. When it is impeded by other constitutional elements, the natural progress of events may be postponed for a time; but in the end the outcome is inevitable. Recent examples of this tendency in practice are the tyrannies of Mussolini's Italy, Hitler's Germany, Mugabe's Zimbabwe and Putin's Russia.

> 'Aren't the people always in the habit of setting up one man as their special champion, nurturing him and making him great?... When a tyrant arises, this special leadership is the sole root from which he sprouts.'
> [Plato "Republic" (VIII 565d)]

Democracy institutionalises conflict

In as far as "fairness" is to be required in politics, Democracy is very much to be avoided; for Democracy[9] is apt to produce stable voting blocks which get all their own way: effectively excluding even large minorities from any exercise of power. This can easily lead to understandable feelings of "social exclusion" and "marginalization", and result in societal disintegration leading to disorder, violence and rebellion.

Democracy[9] is characterized by ongoing conflict. Temporary closure is provided by a vote which is won by one faction at the expense of all others; but this obtains neither consensus nor any other obvious benefit: rather, it tends to fuel resentment. Partisan Democracy is in fact predicated on the idea that consensus is impossible; and that the best which can be hoped for is that "my side" will obtain power – at least for a time.

---

8   The derogatory term "populist" is often applied to political parties with supposedly "extremist" policies which have significant support among those elements of society deemed to be less educated by the political establishment and/or media.

9   In the sense of the rule of the popular majority.

Politics is too important for Democracy

In matters of little importance, it may be that everyone in society is content that decisions are made according to majority vote. After all, those who do not "get their way" are not going to be very committed to their preference, and will easily come to terms with whatever is decided. On the other hand, it might be just as appropriate to decide such matters by lottery or by the diktat of a leader. In such matters, it really doesn't matter what is decided or how it is done. If this is done democratically, so be it; if not, who is going to care?

If a wrong decision is made in some matter of great import, then everyone – or at least a lot of people – will suffer. It is supremely unimportant *how* the decision is made, or *by whom*; but only that the *right* decision is made. It will be no consolation to anyone that what was decided was what the majority desired – or even that it was a consensus – if the decision turned out to be *wrong*. Equally, no reasonable person would complain if a corrupt, excessively partisan, or ineffectual democratic government was overturned by a coup, in a moment of emergency; and the nation saved by the decisive actions of a wise and responsible military dictator.

In matters of moderate import the situation becomes unclear. People care about the outcome; and will not be content to go along with whatever is decided, even if the decision seems to result in a favourable outcome. They will argue that their idea would have resulted in an even better outcome, and feel aggrieved that they did not get their way. What is required here is consensus: not on every individual matter – realistically this is not going to obtained! – but on a *process* to be used to decide who's policy should prevail. As long as this *process* is agreed by consensus, its details are of no account. In particular, Democracy[9] has nothing obvious to recommend it; though it would serve well enough.

Political decisions regularly matter. They can involve questions of war and peace, prosperity and poverty, freedom and oppression, and the conservation or despoliation of the planet. These are all issues where technical expertise and calm, wise and measured judgement count. They are issues regarding which the massed population is ignorant.[10]

This is, indeed, the basis on which referenda are disapproved of by the British political establishment. The idea being that the general public is incompetent to decide such issues by majority vote; and so should leave such matters to the expert judgement of the political class. This is manifestly absurd; for the political class which presents this argument is itself founded on – and takes its sole legitimacy from – the democratic process: its characteristic expertise being nothing more than the ability to lie persuasively.

It is, of course, similarly absurd to determine political questions by the majority vote of elected politicians; which is why, in spite of themselves, UK politicians have handed off some political decisions to agencies which are only remotely controlled by government. The prime example is the Bank of England, which now has control of monetary policy.

Mob rule

Behind all of Plato's theoretical objections to Democracy stands the historical fact that the Athenian democrats had Socrates tried and executed for "corrupting the youth". This conclusively demonstrated to Plato the basic injustice of Democracy, which he thought amounted to mob rule.

In the end, the common people are typically most interested in their short-term personal standard of living. They are swayed by hand-outs of free bread; warnings about foreign threats and the promise of "peace in our time". They rise to the denunciation of "bogus asylum seekers", "terrorists", "fat cats", "scroungers", and "child molesters". They rally to the flag when carried aloft by some sports team or other.

---

10 The author wishes to make it clear that he includes himself within "the massed population" and claims no personal expertise in matters of state. This book is in no way a personal manifesto or bid to obtain political power!

'One part is this class of idlers, that grows... because of the general permissiveness... in a Democracy... this class[11] is the dominant one. Then there's a second class... [in which] everybody is trying to make money, those who are naturally most organized generally become the wealthiest...

The "people" – those who work with their own hands – are the third class. They take no part in politics... but, when they are assembled, they are the largest and most powerful class in a Democracy... but they aren't willing to assemble often unless they get a share of the money... and they always do, though the leaders, in taking the wealth of the rich and distributing it to the people, keep the greater part for themselves...

The people act as they do because they are ignorant and are deceived by the drones, and the rich act as they do because they are driven to it by the stinging of the same drones.'

[Plato "Republic" (VIII 565a-c)]

An initial problem

There is an obvious problem here. It is not clear what expertise a good ruler ought to have – apart from the impossible expertise of being a universal oracle! – or how those who are to be ruled would be able to judge whether a potential ruler had this expertise.

Whereas doctors hold a generally large consensus about what the best route of curing a person might be, political theorists and governors do not. I am not sure how strong the analogy is. For example, supposing philosophy were to be taught in grade school – would you want a board of modern philosophers voting on what ought to be taught as the best methods of philosophy?

[J. Kramer "Private Communication" (2015)]

---

11 Professional politicians: "Drones".

It seems to me that the minimal characteristics of a good ruler are: first, the ability to discern expertise in others; second, the willingness to delegate decision making in various fields to those judged to be competent in those fields; and third, the ability to discern whether others are noble of heart or else corrupt. Plato asserts that the third characteristic is not so difficult to attain; and that most persons of a normal level of intelligence would be able to judge the morality of others by secretly observing how they behave in situations involving ethical dilemmas.[12] The second characteristic is a combination of humility and faith and, though not common, is hardly exceptional or superhuman.

The problematic characteristic is the first; for on what possible basis could a generalist ever be competent to judge the expert competence of a specialist? Arguably, this is the kernel of the virtue called discernment: the ability to penetrate to the root of things, bypassing all incidental details. This expertise can be developed by cultivating the Socratic method of asking those who claim understanding of certain matters penetrating questions pertinent to their supposed knowledge, and of listening carefully to their responses: to see whether these are not only self consistent but also correspond with observation, experience, and – if possible – experiment.

In the realms of warfare, diplomacy, economics, criminology, education, sociology (and indeed all the so-called "social sciences") those people who claim expertise disagree with each other: holding to divergent theories which are constitutionally incapable of being tested scientifically. Hence it is a forlorn task for even the most discerning of rulers to definitively determine which putative expert(s) ought to be allowed to set policy in any of the fields which are the proper business of the state. Nevertheless, some choice has to be made by some agent or agency, and to neglect to make any such choice is itself a choice.

As to Kramer's specific question I would certainly not "want a board of modern philosophers voting on what ought to be taught as the best methods of philosophy"! This is because I personally believe that the preponderance of "modern philosophers" have

---

12 Plato "Republic" (III 412e-413c), quoted on page 46.

departed very far from the proper business of philosophy. However – changing Kramer's question – I would be very happy to have a board of classical philosophers deciding (by vote or otherwise) on the ministerial composition of a governing council of state.

Ch 6   The Philosopher King

'The whole point of our legislation was to allow the citizens to live supremely happy lives in the greatest possible mutual friendship.' [Plato "Laws" (V 743d)]

Plato bases his politics on the notion that friendship is the foundation of society. He considers the ideal situation, where conflict is absent because the populace are united by real benevolence towards each other; sharing a common vision and purpose that is based on a deep knowledge of justice, beauty and goodness. This is contrary to the modern view, which takes for granted the existence of discord, and seeks only to find a way of managing or defusing it. Modern commentators too easily misinterpret Plato's ideas as proposals for suppressing conflict and imposing an artificial monolithic uniformity.

'How does Plato solve the problem of avoiding class war? Had he been a progressivist, he might have hit on the idea of a classless, equalitarian society... But he was not out to construct a state that might come, but a state that had been – the father of the Spartan state, which was certainly not a classless society. It was a slave state, and accordingly Plato's best state is based on the most rigid class distinctions. It is a caste state. The problem of avoiding class war is solved, not by abolishing classes, but by giving the ruling class a superiority which cannot be challenged.'
[K.R. Popper "The Spell of Plato" Ch 4 (1945)]

This is to misrepresent Plato's purpose. Indeed, he proposes that a certain moderation between the excesses of authoritarianism and libertarianism is characteristic of the ideal state.

'We have reviewed a moderate authoritarianism and a moderate freedom and saw the results: tremendous progress in each case; but when either the Persians

or the Athenians pushed things to extremes – of subjugation in the one case and its opposite in the other – it did neither of them any good at all.'
[Plato "Laws" (III 701e)]

Moreover, it cannot be emphasized too much that Plato is concerned to establish friendship among all the citizens, and not just among the elite rulers. Moreover, he nowhere categorizes the working and merchant class as slaves.

He does not deny education to any-one. In fact he emphasizes the role which education and play should have in revealing those individuals who have dispositions which fit them to fill positions of authority.

'Education must be compulsory, "for every man and boy", because they belong to the state first and their parents second... so far as possible... the female sex should be on the same footing as the male.'
[Plato "Laws" (VII 804d, 805d)]

'We must observe them at all ages to see whether they are guardians of this conviction [that they must eagerly pursue what is advantageous to the city] and make sure that neither compulsion nor magic spells will get them to disregard or forget their belief that they must do what is best for the city... We must... set them tasks that are most likely to make them forget such a conviction or be deceived out of it, and we must select whoever keeps on remembering it and isn't easily deceived, and reject the others.'
[Plato "Republic" (III 412e-413c)]

'Nothing taught by force stays in the soul... don't use force to train the children... use play instead. That way you'll also see better what each of them is naturally fitted for.' [Plato "Republic" (VII 536e)]

Plato certainly did look back in history for guidance as to the form of the ideal state; however, he was not an antiquarian: concerned to dig up and reconstruct ancient ruins. He was rather concerned with clarifying the target for which we should be aiming in politics. He thought that if we have some kind of vision we might make progress towards it. He knew that if we do not we will simply flounder around aimlessly.

'Perhaps... there is a model of it in heaven, for anyone who wants to look at it and to make himself its citizen on the strength of what he sees.'
[Plato "Republic" (IX 592b)]

Although the ideal state has never existed on Earth in the past, and may never exist on Earth in the future; yet this Kingdom still calls us onwards and upwards – promising a lifestyle and quality of fellowship worthy of mankind's noble potential.

The role of law

Plato subjugates all law to the cultivation of virtue, and thereby justice; which will produce friendship and general happiness.

'Keep a sharp eye on this present legislation, in case I lay down some law which is not conducive to virtue, or which fosters only a part of it.'
[Plato "Laws" (IV 705e)]

For Plato, the sole end of governance is the establishment of justice on a shared understanding of what is objectively good.

'No matter how states or individuals think that they can achieve the good, it is a conception of what the good is that should govern every man and hold sway in his soul, even if he is a little mistaken.'
[Plato "Laws" (IX 864a)]

Plato insists that law should always be explained to the populace at large.

'Should the regulations appear in the light of a loving and prudent father and mother? Or should they act the tyrant and despot, posting their orders and threats on walls and leaving it at that?'
[Plato "Laws" (IX 859a)]

The best law is advisory and instructional, but some law serves the purpose of reigning in vice.

'Some laws, it seems, are made for the benefit of honest men, to teach them the rules of association that have to be observed if they are to live in friendship; others are made for those who refuse to be instructed and whose naturally tough natures have not been softened enough to stop them turning to absolute vice.'
[Plato "Laws" (IX 880e)]

The necessity of such law is regrettable, but inevitable – given the concupiscence present in humanity.

'The mere idea that a state[1] of this kind could give rise to a man affected by the worst forms of wickedness found in other countries... is in a way a disgrace... we have to lay down laws against these people... when they appear, on the assumption that they will certainly do so... we are not framing laws for heroes and sons of gods... but we are human beings, legislating in the world today for the children of men, and we shall give no offence by our fear that one of our citizens will turn out to... resist   softening;   powerful   as   our   laws   are, they may not be able to tame such people.'
[Plato "Laws" (IX 853c-d)]

---

1   Here "state" clearly means "society" itself, rather than the governing mechanisms and institutions of society.

The just ruler

Plato argues that most people need to be ruled, taught, managed and directed; and that at best only a few are competent to exercise these functions.

'We say that he ought to be the slave of that best person who has a divine ruler within himself. It isn't to harm the slave that we say he must be ruled (which is what Thrasymachus thought to be true of all subjects) but because it is better for everyone to be ruled by divine reason – preferably within himself and his own, otherwise imposed from without – so that as far as possible all will be alike and friends, governed by the same thing.'
[Plato "Republic" (IX 590d)]

Rulers should not be motivated by a craving for power.

'A city whose prospective rulers are least eager to rule must of necessity be most free from civil war, whereas a city with the opposite kind of rulers is governed in the opposite way.'
[Plato "Republic" (VII 520d)]

Rather, they should be sought out and, when found, be begged to take up the responsibility of governance. This is almost the antithesis of Representative Democracy.

'The natural thing is... for anyone who needs to be ruled is to knock at the door of the one who can rule him. It isn't for the ruler, if he's truly any use, to beg the others to accept his rule.' [Plato "Republic" (VI 489c)]

Plato argues that the ideal form of government would be that of a benign and just absolute dictator, concerned only for the common good and unconstrained by any constitutional limitations. However, he admits that this is a long shot and proposes, as second best, a state based on a written constitution.

'If ever, by the grace of God, some natural genius were
born, and had the chance to assume [the rule of the state]
he would have no need of laws to control him.
Knowledge is unsurpassed by any law or regulation;
reason, if it is genuine and really enjoys its natural
freedom, should have universal power... but as it is,
such a character is nowhere to be found, except a hint
of it here and there. That is why we need to choose the
second alternative: law and regulation.'
[Plato "Laws" (IX 875c-d)]

Constitutional law exists to limit the freedom of those fallible
mortals who govern and administer the affairs of the state,
directing them towards an interest in the common good. Statute
law exists to harmonize the activities of its citizens.[2]

Plato insisted that rulers should personally identify with the
good of all, be tenacious in pursuing what is true and just,
and have a fundamental and unswerving loyalty towards the state,
based on the rational belief that co-operation and kindness are in
their own self-interest.

'Mustn't they be knowledgeable and capable, and mustn't
they care for the city?' [Plato "Republic" (III 412c)]

Only in this way can a commitment to the common good be
justified and maintained.

'Someone loves something most of all when he believes
that the same things are advantageous to it as to himself,
and supposes that if it does well, he'll do well, and that
if it does badly, then he'll do badly too.'
[Plato "Republic" (III 412d)]

He proposed that commitment to the common good should be
reinforced by forbidding the rulers personal wealth, and allowing
them to hold possessions only in common, like monastics.

---

2   Plato "Laws" (IX 880e), quoted on page 48.

'Guardians... mustn't have private houses, property
or possessions, but must receive their upkeep from
the other citizens as a wage for their guardianship
and enjoy it in common.' [Plato "Republic" (V 464c)]

For Plato, patriotism is based on a vision of a state that is
constituted – and its affairs conducted – in accordance with
justice. If the state deviates from this it looses any call on the
loyalty of its citizens.

'Our aim in life should be goodness and the spiritual
virtue appropriate to mankind... Rather than have the
state... be ruled by unworthy hands, it may be absolutely
necessary to allow it to be destroyed... rather than permit
a change to the sort of political system which will make
men worse.' [Plato "Laws" (VI 770d-e)]

Plato contrasts the true king: who is concerned with justice,
and is happy; with the tyrant: who is driven by desire for what
he wants, and is wretched.

'The best, the most just, and the most happy is the most
kingly, who rules like a king over himself, and the worst,
the most unjust and the most wretched is the most
tyrannical, who most tyrannized himself and the city
he rules.' [Plato "Republic" (IX 580c)]

On the basis that the "kingly man" is clearly a lover of
wisdom, he concludes that only philosophers are qualified to hold
positions of governance or administration.

'Until philosophers rule as kings, or those who are now
called kings and leading men genuinely and adequately
philosophize... cities will have no rest from evils...
nor will the human race.' [Plato "Republic" (V 473c-d)]

Ch 7   The case against Plato

'Indiscriminate equality for all amounts to inequality...
We use the same term for two concepts of "equality",
which in most respects are virtual opposites. The first sort
– of measures and weights and numbers – is within the
competence of any state... but the most genuine
equality... needs the wisdom and judgement of Zeus...

The general method I mean is to give much to the
great and less to the less great, adjusting what you give to
take account of the real nature of each... statesmanship
consists of essentially this – strict justice...

The founder of any state should... take no account of
a bunch of dictators, or a single one, or even the power
of the people. He must always make justice his aim...
it consists of granting the "equality" that unequals deserve
to get.' [Plato "Laws" (VI 757b-d)]

Plato is often presented as an advocate for a totalitarian society.
This is mainly because in his great work "Republic" he seems
to propose a form of elitist governance best described as the rule
of philosopher guardians. His political vision was based on his
idea of justice: that harmonious state of affairs in which everyone
is allowed to mind his own proper business and hence to fulfil
their potential, freely and peaceably collaborating together
as friends; with the outcome that the common good is served.

'Justice brings friendship and a sense of common
purpose.' [Plato "Republic" (I 351d)]

'Justice is doing one's own work and not meddling with
what isn't one's own.' [Plato "Republic" (IV 433a)]

He is hostile to the concept of "social equality", dismissing
it as irrational. He praises the contrary practice of conferring
recognition and responsibility on those persons of virtue,
and passing over the mass of the population as of lesser account.

This principle is also found in the following parable of Jesus of Nazareth.

> 'When he returned, having received the kingdom, he commanded these servants, to whom he had given the money, to be called to him; that he might know what they had gained by trading. The first came before him, saying, "Lord, your pound has made ten pounds more."
>
> And he said to him, "Well done, good servant! Because you have been faithful in a very little, you shall have authority over ten cities."...
>
> Then another came, saying, "Lord, here is your pound, which I kept laid away in a napkin."...
>
> And he said to those who stood by, "Take the pound from him, and give it to him who has the ten pounds... I tell you, that to every one who has will more be given; but from him who has not, even what he has will be taken away."' [Lk 19: 15-26 RSV]

This is strictly rational and fair. Those who have competence in some matter should be given responsibility in that matter, so that they can make free use of their ability. Those who are generally incompetent should be kept well away from all power. This contrasts starkly with a more modern, conventional, and liberal concept of justice which takes it for granted that all have equal ability and that the only thing that anyone can lack is the opportunity to demonstrate their talent.

The humanitarian theory of justice makes three main demands or proposals, namely (a) the equalitarian principle proper, i.e. the proposal to eliminate 'natural' privileges, (b) the general principle of individualism, and (c) the principle that it should be the task and the purpose of the state to protect the freedom of its citizens. To each of these political demands or proposals there corresponds a directly opposite principle of Platonism, namely (a1) the principle of natural privilege, (b2) the general principle of holism or collectivism,

and (c1) the principle that it should be the task and the purpose of the individual to maintain, and to strengthen, the stability of the state.
[K.R. Popper "The Spell of Plato" Ch 6 (1945)]

Many of the specific political ideas that Plato details in his "Republic" are offensive to modern ears. In particular, he seems to legitimize state propaganda;[1] recommends strict censorship of the arts;[2] and insists on state control of education.[3] He also gives the appearance of being a conservative reactionary[4] and, worse, he sponsors a revolutionary form of communism, involving the total abolition of the family.[5] To top it all, Plato combines this with the introduction of a clandestine breeding programme aimed at continually improving the genetic stock of the population.[6]

---

1   "If it is appropriate for anyone to use falsehoods for the good of the city... it is the rulers." [Plato "Republic" (III 389b)]
2   "We certainly won't... allow it to be said that... any hero and son of a god dared to do any of the terrible and impious deeds that they are now falsely said to have done. We'll compel the poets either to deny that the heroes did such things, or else to deny that they were children of the gods. They mustn't say both." [Plato "Republic" (III 391c-d)]
3   "Those in charge must cling to education and see that it isn't corrupted without their noticing it, guarding it against everything. Above all, they must guard as carefully as they can against any innovation in music and poetry or in physical training that is counter to the established order." [Plato "Republic" (IV 424b)]
4   Plato "Laws" (VII 797d) quoted on page 59.
5   "If by being well educated they become reasonable men, they will easily see these things for themselves.... That marriage, the having of wives, and the procreation of children must be governed as far as possible by the old proverb: 'Friends possess everything in common.'" [Plato "Republic" (IV 423e)]
6   'First, the best men must have sex with the best women as frequently as possible, while the opposite is true of the most inferior men and women; and, second... the former's offspring must be reared but not the latter's. This must all be brought about without being noticed by anyone.' [Plato "Republic" (V 459d-e)]

It is not clear how committed Plato was to all (or any) of these proposals; and even less clear that he believed that they were of any practical application, baring miraculous intervention.

'No city, constitution, or individual man will ever become perfect until either some chance event compels those few philosophers who aren't vicious... to take charge of a city... and compels the city to obey them, or until a god inspires the present rulers and kings or their offspring with a true erotic love for true philosophy.'
[Plato "Republic" (VI 499b)]

'One such individual would be sufficient to bring to completion all the things that now seem so incredible, providing that his city obeys him.
[Plato "Republic" (VI 502b)]

At the end of his life, Plato revisited the question of the ideal state, writing a second dialogue "Laws", in which he offers an alternate account, based on constitutional law. He still expresses a preference for a type of communism;[7] but doubts that it is practical, and proposes as second best a state in which both extreme poverty and extreme affluence are made impossible.[8]

Answering Plato's critics

Plato is not a proponent of demagogy. He insists that only philosophers with a genuine concern for the common good, should rule. His purpose is to make all the citizens of his state friends, and both virtuous and happy. His politics is clearly distinguished from "totalitarianism" by these aims, and his insistence on the rule of justice. In spite of this, Popper asserts:

I believe that Plato's political programme, far from being morally superior to totalitarianism, is fundamentally identical with it. I believe that the objections against this

7   Plato "Laws" (V 739c)
8   Plato "Laws" (V 739d-744b)

view are based upon an ancient and deep-rooted prejudice in favour of idealizing Plato… It is interesting that this tendency could persist for such a long time in spite of the fact that Grote and Gomperz had pointed out the reactionary character of some doctrines of the Republic and the Laws. But even they did not see all the implications of these doctrines; they never doubted that Plato was, fundamentally, a humanitarian. And their adverse criticism was ignored, or interpreted as a failure to understand and to appreciate Plato who was by Christians considered a 'Christian before Christ', and by revolutionaries a revolutionary.
[K.R. Popper "The Spell of Plato" Ch6 (1945)]

This is nothing more than a manifestation of Popper's own principle that what one sees in a thing is heavily influenced by what one expects to find there. Those who come to Plato hoping to find humility, truth, beauty and compassion, will be richly rewarded. They will place his rigour within the context of an absolute dedication to the search for truth and justice, which had yet only just been begun. Those who come to Plato fearing to find conceit, and intolerance, will also find what they seek.[9]

Plato was not a Liberal. He believed in objective reality and in truth. He was not a Libertarian. He believed in the value of friendship, partnership and co-operation; and in the rule of just laws. He was not a Progressivist. He believed that change was, of itself, regrettable.[10] None of these facts are failings. All of Plato's specific legislative proposals were intended to advance virtue, justice and fellowship. In as far as they do not objectively do so, he would have us ignore them.[11]

---

9 Popper's view of Plato is heavily coloured first, by the terrible experience of Nazism and Marxism, note the date of publication of "The Spell of Plato"; and second, by his idea that all political systems were either "democratic" or "tyrannical". On this basis Plato is clearly a champion of "Popperian tyranny", even though Plato regularly condemns tyranny as the very worst form of governance.
10 Plato "Laws" (VII 797d), quoted above.
11 Plato "Laws" (IV 705e) quoted on page 47.

Some of Plato's proposals may be dismissed out of hand as absurd or impractical; but in most, if not all, there lies a kernel of truth. Plato was undoubtedly right that family, clan and tribe are to various extents opposed to the formation of a stable and harmonious civil society. He argues that his alternate set of social institutions would break down kinship barriers within society, and give everyone an equal affiliation within the community. He concludes that this would bring about the great good of a sense of commonality, co-responsibility and corporate identity.

> 'In our city... they'll speak in unison... when any one of them is doing well or badly, they'll say "mine" is doing well or that "mine" is doing badly... the cause of this is the having of wives and children in common.'
> [Plato "Republic" (V 463e-464a)]

Plato and the family

Plato's proposals for the destruction of family may seem inhumane; but if we reject them, we must somehow answer the charge which Plato addresses to us: "How will you tame the family? How will we render it the servant of friendship and of society, rather then their enemy?" Jesus of Nazareth offers us the same challenge.

> Now great multitudes accompanied him; and He turned and said to them, 'If any one comes to Me and does not hate[12] his own father and mother and wife and children and brothers and sisters, yes, and even his own life, he cannot be My disciple.' [Lk. 14:25-26 RSV]

---

12 This is an example of Semitic hyperbole. Jesus does not mean His followers to hate any-one and certainly not their own lives! What He means is that we must have an accurate view of the relative importance of things and that family, material possessions and one's mortal existence are of no consequence compared to eternity.

Moreover, He offers a solution which is similar to Plato's:

> And his mother and his brothers came; and standing outside they sent to him and called him. And a crowd was sitting about him; and they said to him, 'Your mother and your brothers are outside, asking for you.'
> And he replied, 'Who are my mother and my brothers?' And looking around on those who sat about him, he said, 'Here are my mother and my brothers! Whoever does the will of God is my brother, and sister, and mother.' [Mk 3:31-35 RSV]

Plato's eugenics

As for Plato's eugenic breeding programme, it has at least the virtue of consistency. If sex is for procreation then it should be organized for the best procreative outcome; and it would be difficult to think of a system more suited to this end than the one proposed by Plato in "Republic". Moreover, Plato does not include such a scheme in his more mature work, "Laws", beyond the statute "If a couple remain childless... they should part... and decide terms of divorce."[13] I suppose the reason that Plato gave up on eugenics was that he was unable to think how a programme could be implemented without doing more harm to society (by institutionalizing either coercion or dishonesty) than good.

Plato's conservatism

Plato's aversion to change and all challenge to the "status quo" of the ideal state is based on the fact that the ideal state is already perfect and so can only be degraded by change.

> 'Change... except in something evil, is extremely dangerous.' [Plato "Laws" (VII 797d)]

---

13 Plato "Laws" (VI 784b)

Of course, there never has been such a state; and Plato was not adverse to unjust rulers being criticized, challenged, denounced or deposed. Indeed, it was Socrates' unrelenting implicit challenge to the rulers of his day that attracted their ire and led to his death.

The idea that Plato could be opposed to charitable free speech is absurd. His entire method is based on remorseless – but impersonal – criticism. In his dialogues, he regularly has Socrates invite his opponents, colleagues and pupils to put forward their own views, no matter how ill advised or absurd. Socrates also expects them, as his equals on the journey towards enlightenment, to challenge the theories and proposals that he puts forward.[14]

> 'I'll be very grateful.... to you if you refute me and rid me of this nonsense. Please don't falter now in doing a friend a good turn. Refute me.' [Plato Gorgias (470c)]

The only thing that Plato will not tolerate and make place for is manifest ill will.

Plato's conceit

Popper criticizes Plato's idea of "the philosopher king" on the basis that Plato constructed it so as to proclaim himself Emperor of All. Now, while this might have been no bad thing, in practice Plato never attempted to seize power for himself. Instead, he recommended that any person who approximated to the form of the true philosopher should avoid playing any part in politics and instead live a life of obscurity.

> 'Then there remains, Adeimantus, only a very small group who consort with philosophy in a way that's worthy of her: a noble and well brought-up character, for example, kept down by exile, who remains with philosophy according to his nature because there is no one to corrupt him, or a great soul living in a small city, who dislikes the city's affairs and looks beyond them...

---

14 Plato "Gorgias" (506a) quoted on p62.

Now the members of this small group have tasted how sweet and blessed a possession philosophy is, and at the same time they've also seen the madness of the majority and realized, in a word, that hardly anyone acts sanely in public affairs and that there is no ally with whom they might go to the aid of justice and survive, that instead they'd perish before they could profit either their city or their friends and be useless both to themselves and to others... taking all this into account, they live a quiet life and do their own work... the philosopher... is satisfied if he can somehow lead his present life free from injustice and impious acts and depart from it with good hope, blameless and content.' [Plato "Republic" (VI 496a-e)]

Moreover, Popper's attack appropriates Plato's own values, captured in his characterization of Socrates.

'What a monument of human smallness is this idea of the philosopher king. What a contrast between it and the simplicity and humaneness of Socrates, who warned the statesmen against the danger of being dazzled by his own power, excellence, and wisdom, and who tried to teach him what matters most – that we are all frail human beings. What a decline from this world of irony and reason and truthfulness down to Plato's kingdom of the sage whose magical powers raise him high above ordinary men; although not quite high enough to forgo the use of lies, or to neglect the sorry trade of every shaman – the selling of spells, of breeding spells, in exchange for power over his fellow-men.'
[K.R. Popper "The Spell of Plato" Ch 8 (1945)]

This is absurd. It is precisely the fact that Plato held these values dear that should guide us when interpreting his writings. Sometimes, as a frail human being, he may deviate from them. Where it seems clear that he does so, we must reject what he says. We do no disservice to him in this. After all, he explicitly tells us to do just this, in the person of Socrates.

'Give but little thought to Socrates, but much more to the truth. If you think that what I say is true, agree with me; if not, oppose it with every argument and take care that in my eagerness I do not deceive myself and you.'
[Plato "Phaedo" (91c)]

Moreover, Plato regularly has his protagonists disclaim any expert knowledge of anything!

'The things I say I certainly don't say with any knowledge at all; no, I'm searching together with you so that if my opponent clearly has a point, I'll be the first to concede it.' [Plato "Gorgias" (506a)]

'I am far, by Zeus, from believing that I know the cause of any of those things. I will not even allow myself to say that where one is added to one, either the one to which it is added or the one that is added become two.'
[Plato "Phaedo" (96e)]

We should also recall that not everything that Plato seems to recommend should be taken at face value. I am convinced that many of his ideas are proposed solely for the purpose of being criticized, while others are deeply ironic.

The basic problem

The standard critique of Plato's system of "philosopher guardians" is summarized in Juvanal's quip "who will watch the warders?"[15] This is based on a misunderstanding of what Plato is proposing. Simply put: if the guardians were to be of the character that Plato stipulates in "Republic" they would not need any guarding. Juvakal's question presumes that the "wardens" are only *relatively* good, and so still prone to vice. This is the more realistic case that Plato addresses in "Laws", where he proposes that a written constitution might serve the purpose of "guarding

---

15 Juvinal "Satires" (VI 347–8)

the council of guardians"; so long as those in positions of governance and administration were *sufficiently* virtuous.

Unfortunately, both of Plato's solutions to the problem of politics (that is "Republic" and "Laws") rely on access to objective justice: in the person of a wise monarch, a meritocracy of virtuous philosopher guardians, or the text of a good written constitution.[16] This is the real deficit in his case. Because this is such a fundamental deficit, it is no reason to reject Plato's programme. The same deficit will be found in all systems of governance.[17] At least in Plato's politics the difficulty is placed openly in the lime-light.

The same defect in any external code is implicit in the prophecy of Jeremiah:

> Behold, the days come, saith the LORD, that I will make a new covenant with the house of Israel, and with the house of Judah: not according to the covenant that I made with their fathers... which... they brake...
>
> But this shall be the covenant that I will make with the house of Israel... I will put my law in their inward parts, and write it in their hearts... And they shall teach no more every man his neighbour, and every man his brother, saying: "Know the LORD!"; for they shall all know me, from the least of them unto the greatest of them.
> [Jer 31:31-34 KJV]

The key to just government is not any system of governance (not even a divinely inspired system, and certainly not Democracy!) but a transformation of the hearts of those governed. Until the people all "know the LORD" as a matter of heart-felt understanding: that is, until they each possess interior justice,

---

16 Not merely objective justice in any narrow sense; but a real expertise in every aspect of good governance and statesmanship.

17 Marx, for example, assumes that in the end there would be no need for the proletariat to be coerced into conformity; as they will all eventually come to want to do what is politically correct from an internal sense of community.

no externally applied system can serve to humanise them and make them behave reasonably with kindness, equity and mercy.

Finished your draft,[18] really enjoyed it. It was something of a new idea to me, but one obvious when I thought about it – the best kind! If not totally convinced, I'm most of the way convinced that it always comes down to the quality of the people governing and being governed, and not the system in place. Thanks for sending it to me.

I have already been bringing this up in political discussions recently, to some startling success. Most people seem to recognize the clarity of the argument immediately. We must all be clouded up with too much talk of political theories and what not!

[J. Kramer "Private Communication" (2015)]

---

18 Kramer had kindly agreed to read-through an early version of this pamphlet.

Ch 8   A sketched proposal

'A system of selection like that will effect a compromise between a monarchical and a democratic constitution, which is precisely the sort of compromise a constitution should always be.' [Plato "Laws" (VI 756e)]

When faced with a criticism of Democracy, people normally respond with a demand that a better proposal be set forth. Now it is not my primary concern to do this: first, because I believe that the common folk are not at all ready to harken to the idea that they should give up their perceived sovereignty, even for their own advantage; and second, because it is not necessary to have the right answer to a problem in order to see that another answer is wrong. However, so as to make some kind of response to the typical reaction, I will sketch out a few specific ideas in this final chapter.

Plato's dielectic

Plato believed that the process of dialectic would inevitably – though with much travail – result in true understanding of any problem, and hence in its rational resolution. This is the process characteristic of Plato's dialogues, especially the early ones.

In the political arena this amounts to the idea that – after due critique, discussion and debate – various solutions to each problem should be trialled; and that those which in fact fail be rejected, while the one judged to give the best results be adopted. Generally, this amounts to "free market competition"; with the proviso that the phrase "best results" may itself sometimes be ambiguous, or even contentious.

When free market competition is not applicable, the matter in question should be evolved by a cycle of "continual improvement". By such means, the effects of a law, policy, or administrative process can be routinely evaluated, and attempts at improvement made where this is indicated. Once again, however, the standard according to which the effects are to be evaluated may be contentious.

Such a political system is less tidy than any envisaged by Plato; who only really considers the case where the end result of this process is already available. Pending such a conclusion, people of good will are bound to disagree on particulars; even if they happen to agree on all matters of principle. It is not clear that they will even agree on what counts as a good outcome for some policy choices. In such circumstances, the best that can be done is that those judged to be wise should take council together and by a dialectical process of discussion form a view as to what should be done.

There are two further problems. The first is how to ensure that only knowledgeable persons of good will become part of the government. The second is how to react to an urgent threat, where there is no time for extended discussion, and no opportunity to trial alternative responses.

The Academy and the Council

The first problem is a matter of education, and could be addressed in the following way. Those in charge of education (the Academy) would co-opt promising students to their number, as academics – on the basis of their being virtuous, and of a theoretical bent. They would appoint others to the Council of Guardians – on the basis of their being virtuous, and of a practical bent.

The Academy should itself be independent of government, and play no role in government; except that it should have the power to remove someone from the Council of Guardians if they were judged to fail in their duty. All that is required is for an initial Academy to be constituted, and that this set of persons be truly wise, moderate, courageous and just.

Emergency powers

The second problem is more practical than theoretical. If there is insufficient time for due process, then there is no alternative but to constitute some small group (or even an individual dictator, potentially the reigning Monarch) with the task of making executive decisions. They should be chosen as carefully as the situation permits, having every appearance of being wise and just; and their decisions should be subject to review and ratification, according to the normal decision making process, as soon as circumstances allow.

Separation of Powers

One thing vital to any state that would make any pretence of pursuing justice is that there should be a clear separation of powers, as is typified in the constitution of the United States of America.[1] In particular, it is most important that the judiciary should be independent of both the executive and the legislature.

There is no good reason why the executive should be an adjunct of the legislature, as became true of the British system under Hanoverian rule. Still less is it healthy for the legislature to be a creature of the executive, as became true in the UK during the Blair premiership. USA style political grid-lock is much to be preferred over sectarian rule.

A free parliament and a written constitution

Because there is no infallible means of promoting justice and goodness, the best that can be done is to enshrine these objectives in a written constitution, as clearly as possible; and rely on a system of checks and balances to prevent any single interest group from gaining sway over society as a whole.

The form of the written constitution must be determined by the end that is to be pursued by the state. If this is to be justice, then what really matters is the sustenance of a real dialogue

---

1 The notion of a professional civil service has much to recommend it.

and friendly interchange of ideas between well educated peers. Only on this basis can a consensus be achieved as to the means by which justice should be pursued. Confrontational party politics is inimical to any such process. Hence, some form of non partisan parliament (place of conversation) is much to be preferred over the partisan legislatures typical of modern democracies.

This is not as unrealistic idea as it may sound. The British House of Lords is considerably less confrontational, and much more conversational than the House of Commons.[2] Moreover, the House of Commons was at first non-partisan. Even now, the myth that Members of the House of Commons are elected as individual constituency representatives (rather than as party candidates) is maintained in the practice of allowing the occasional "honourable member" to "cross the chamber" without resubmitting themselves to the electorate.

Constitutional Monarchy

Plato was no exponent of Democracy, yet even he came to accept that a practical state must have democratic mechanisms within its systems of accountability; to act as a pressure release mechanism, if for no other purpose. Personally, I favour a political system having hereditary, meritocratic and democratic elements. Each of these has its own defects; but when combined they are more inclined towards justice than is any one of them alone.

In such a constitutional monarchy, the sovereign would have real executive power; but this would be limited by the terms of a constitution, which would be interpreted and enforced by a strong and independent meritocratic judiciary. The sovereign and the "Council of Guardians" would be appointed by the Academy on the basis of merit. The Parliament would be partly appointed by the Academy, according to clear meritocratic principles, partly elected, and partly hereditary.

---

2   A good number of peers still decline to belong to any party and sit as independents known as "cross-benchers".

Such a polity is not as implausible as it might at first appear. It is not so very different from the British settlement as it existed in the Victorian Era. In those days, Oxford and Cambridge Universities informally served the role of "the Academy" and the public schools provided elitist education.[3] All that needs to be added is a legislative Senate made up of appointed experts and a consultative Parliament filled with elected "representatives" who would have the sole power of vetoing the budget.

---

3   This system was later enhanced by grammar schools: which provided high quality education for those judged to be able to benefit most from it.

Postscript

After all this analysis and discussion, have we made any progress? Well, we are no closer to establishing justice upon the face of the Earth. In that sense we are still exactly where we started. However, I hope that I have convinced you that what matters in politics is the *ends* pursued – justice, friendship and virtue – rather than (as Popper and other ideological democrats, would have it) the *means* employed.

Bibliography

"**Plato: Complete Works**" ed J.M. Cooper and D.S. Hutchinson, (Indianapolis, IN; Hackett: 1997).

Ch 1

E. Schrödinger "What is Life?"
(Cambridge; The University Press: 1992)
S. Lovatt "The Good of Being"
(Seattle, WA; CreateSpace: 2012)
K.R. Popper "The Poverty of Historicism"
(London; Routledge: 1999)

Ch 3

R.A. Heinlein "The Moon is a harsh mistress"
(London; New English Library: 1979) p232
Charles I "Defence before the House of Commons" (1649)
history.hanover.edu/courses/excerpts/212trial.html
B. Mussolini and G. Gentile "Fascism"
in "The Italian Encyclopaedia" (Rome: 1932)
www.fordham.edu/halsall/mod/mussolini-fascism.html

Ch 4

**K.R. Popper "The Open Society and Its Enemies. Vol 1:
The Spell of Plato"** [Ch4 p45; Ch7 p124]
(Princeton NJ; The University Press: 5th ed 1966)
K.R. Popper "The Logic of Scientific Discovery"
(London; Hutchinson: 2nd Eng ed 10th imp 1980)

Ch 7

**K.R. Popper "The Open Society and Its Enemies. Vol 1:
The Spell of Plato"** [Ch6 p87&94; Ch 8 p155]
(Princeton NJ; The University Press: 5th ed 1966)
Juvinal "Satires" (VI 347–8)
http://www.tertullian.org/fathers/juvenal_satires_06.htm

www.ingramcontent.com/pod-product-compliance
Lightning Source LLC
Chambersburg PA
CBHW070607290526
45790CB00002B/813